jason mraz love is a four letter word

contents

This book was approved by Jason Mraz

Artwork used with the permission of Atlantic Records
© 2012 Atlantic Recording Corporation
Artwork Direction & Design by Greg Burke

Piano/Vocal arrangements by John Nicholas

Cherry Lane Music Company
Director of Publications/Project Editor: Mark Phillips

ISBN 978-1-60378-958-5

Visit our website at www.cherrylaneprint.com

jason mraz love is a four letter word

Jason Mraz spent 22 months on the road promoting *We Sing, We Dance, We Steal Things,* which followed his previous studio albums—the 2002 debut, *Waiting for My Rocket to Come,* and 2005's *Mr. A-Z.* "The tour was a blast and a whirlwind," he says. "I got turned on to the power of the voice and the power of the melody, and it created this desire in me to do it again immediately. Being able to inspire people and take a very simple message global gave me a preview of what that can do. I got home from the tour and thought, 'How can I spread love to the world through this new platform that I have?' That became my starting point for this new album." That album, *Love Is a Four Letter Word,* contains a heartfelt, uplifting collection that explores love's ups and downs, or, as Mraz puts it: "What one does in love to make it work, and what one does in love when it's time to let go."

Mraz had been writing steadily, putting all of his experiences into song. He eventually pared down to the final 12 that appear on his fourth studio album, *Love Is a Four Letter Word.* Recorded at Hollywood's legendary Sunset Sound with producer Joe Chiccarelli (White Stripes, Christina Perri) and a lineup of all-star session musicians, the album's clever arrangements and rich musical textures cushion the diamond-cut clarity of Mraz's pure tenor voice. "I feel like it showcases a variety of moods, from soulful baby-making-jams, to colorful new-jazz, to love-fueled acoustic-guitar-strokery, to rhythmic sunshine-pop," Mraz says. "And lyrically, I wanted the album to have a balance of the sacred and the silly because I want listeners to have both experiences. I want them to be able to go deep, but not get stuck there. I want them to have sunshine, but not get sunburned."

What ties the songs together is their theme. "I had this vision that the album was going to be called *Love* and I was going to talk about love and share love in one way or another," Mraz says. "I thought it was going to be easy because everything I write comes from a place of love, whether it's a new understanding of it, or a retelling of it, or a reawakening to it. But the more I looked at the subject, the more I realized that love almost can't be defined, and who am I to define it anyway? So I went on a journey to try to define the word and be an expression of it in the world."

That journey led to such songs as first single, "I Won't Give Up," an emotional acoustic-driven declaration that has already connected with the public, debuting at No. 1 on *Billboard*'s Digital Songs chart and topping the iTunes "Top Songs" and Hot AC radio charts. "It's about the experience I had with someone in which I had to go dark and let go of a lot things in order to see that I had everything already," Mraz says. Another movingly reflective moment is the hushed song of longing "In Your Hands," as well as "93 Million Miles," in which Mraz finds peace in the realization that you can feel at home in the world no matter where you are.

Fans of Mraz's upbeat, groove-fueled work will appreciate the feel-good "Everything Is Sound," which Mraz says was inspired by his love for Kirtan—a form of devotional call-and-response group singing in Sanskrit. "I had been going to several Kirtans around L.A. and wanted to write something with a bit of a chant in it so that people could just lose themselves a bit," he says. "I like the idea of sneaking some of that Hallelujah into contemporary pop music."

Other highlights include the breezy "Living in the Moment," the earthy story-song "Frank D. Fixer" (inspired by Mraz's grandfather), and the album's horn-driven opener "The Freedom Song," which was written by Seattle singer-songwriter Luc Reynaud. "Luc composed this song with some kids in a shelter in Baton Rouge after Hurricane Katrina and it was released on a CD called *Harmonic Humanity* and sold by homeless people as a way to raise money," Mraz explains. "When I heard it, I wrote to him and asked him if I could sing it for everyone I knew because it's important to keep the message going." During Mraz's 2010 trip to Ghana to work with anti-slavery organization Free the Slaves, he sang "The Freedom Song" at a school whose many students are former child slaves. The group has adopted it as its theme song.

It's that crossroads where music, love, hope, and giving back intersect that makes it all meaningful for Mraz, a dedicated surfer, yogi, and activist. Having worked with the Surfrider Foundation, Free the Slaves, and the True Colors Fund, as well as actively supporting VH1's Save the Music, Free the Children, SPARC (the School of the Performing Arts in the Richmond Community), MusiCares, and Life Rolls On, Mraz recently established the Jason Mraz Foundation to help sustain organizations aligned with his pillars of service, including working to end human trafficking within the human rights arena and promoting human equality, fighting for environment preservation, advocating for the arts and education, and aiding with recovery and assistance.

"My mission is simple: it's to shine a light through music, which can easily be applied to why I sing these songs," Mraz says. "Oftentimes that light is on the very obvious subject of love. This album represents my view of the world and the realization that I am an important part of it in how the choices I make affect other people. But a little bit of love goes a long way, especially on a planet crowded with individuals struggling with seven billion different versions of human triumph and human suffering. When I remember to simply enjoy being where I am, it makes a world of difference."

The Freedom Song

Words and Music by
Luc Reynaud

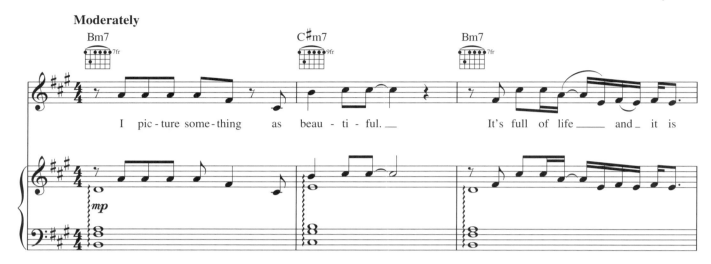

I pic-ture some-thing as beau-ti-ful. It's full of life ___ and ___ it is

all ___ blue. ___ I see a sun-set on the beach, ___ yeah. ___

It makes me feel calm. When I'm calm, I feel ___ good. And
(Good. ___

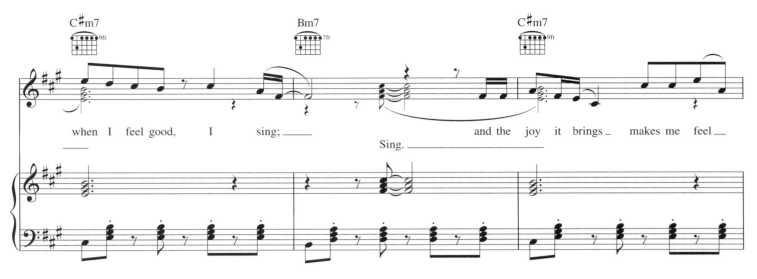

when I feel good, I sing; _____ and the joy it brings _ makes me feel _

_____ Sing. _____

good. And when I feel good, I sing _____ of the

Good. _____ Sing.) _____

Tacet

joy it brings _____ me.

_____

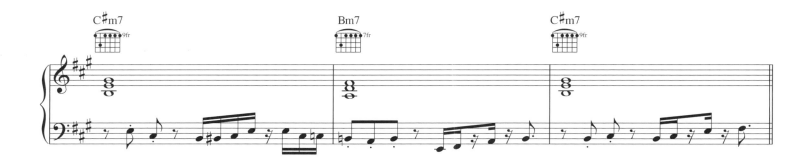

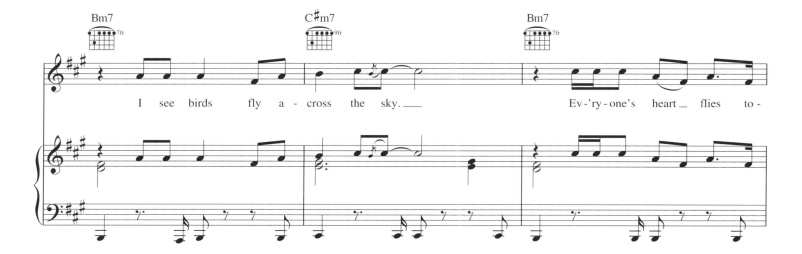

when I feel good, I sing; ___ and the joy it brings ___ makes me feel ___
Sing.

good. And when I ___ feel ___ good, I sing. ___ And the
Good. ___ Sing.) ___

joy it brings... ___ I say: Come on a - long. ___ I know you real - ly wan - na

feel our ___ song. We've got some life to ___ bring. We've got some joy in this thing. ___

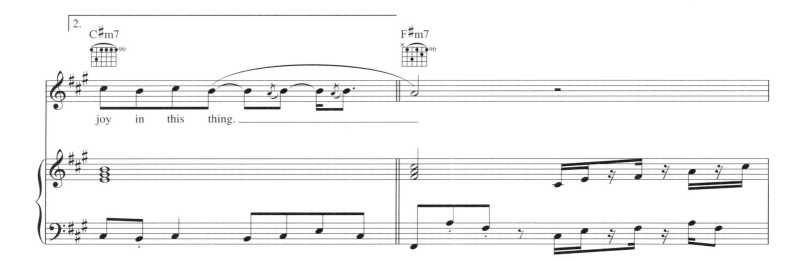

joy in this thing.

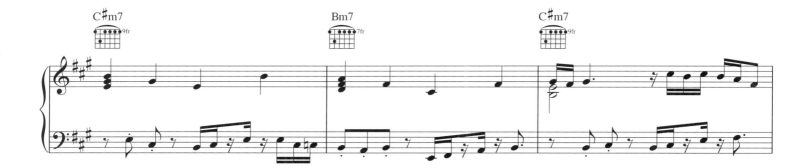

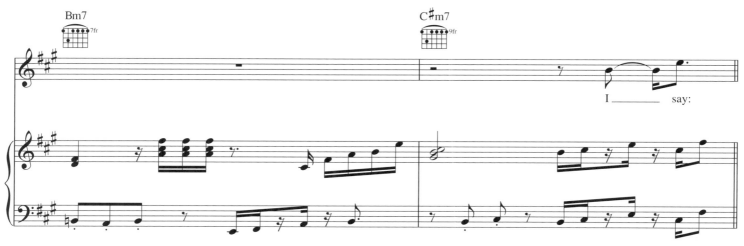

I _____ say:

If you can feel the joy, __ then you should let your-self _____ sing. ___

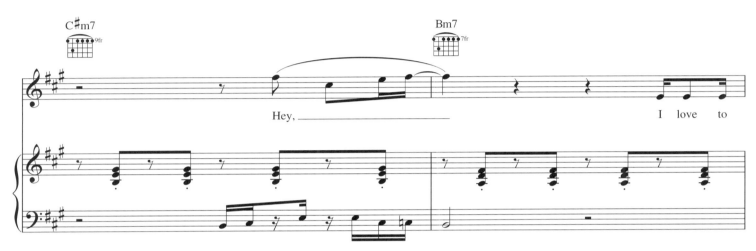

Hey, _____ I love to

share my things __ 'cause it brings me free - dom! (Free - dom! __ Whoa! __

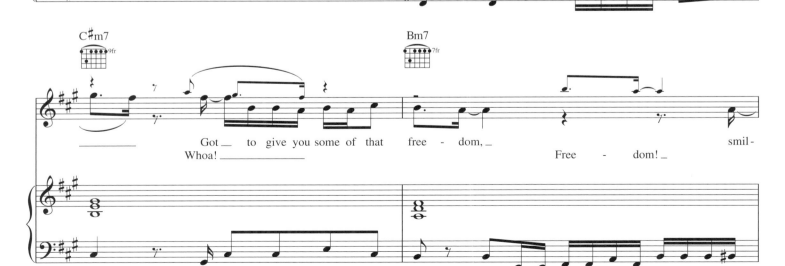

_____ Got __ to give you some of that free - dom, __ Free - dom! __ smil-
Whoa! _____

10

ing and feel-ing your heart beat. Free - dom! Free - dom! Whoa! _

_ You _ de - serve _ your free - dom, _ Free - dom! _ danc-

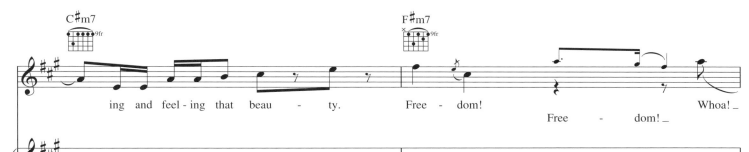

ing and feel-ing that beau - ty. Free - dom! Free - dom! _ Whoa! _

_ Well, it's all for you, all for you,
All for you,

all for you,   all   for you. Sing, free - dom!   Whoa!

all for you,   all   for you. Oh. _____   Free - dom! _

_____   Got   to get - cha some of that, got   to get - cha some of that, got

Whoa!) _____

to get - cha some of that free - dom. _____

Living in the Moment

Words and Music by
Jason Mraz and Rick Nowels

waste my __ days __ mak-ing up all kinds of ways to wor-ry 'bout all the things that will not

hap-pen to me. So I just let go of what I know I don't __ know. __ And I

know I on - ly _____ do this by _____ liv-ing in the

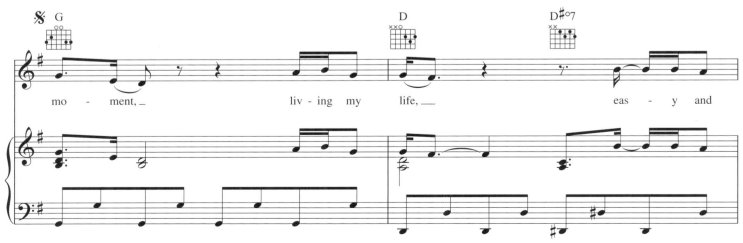

mo - ment, __ liv-ing my life, __ eas - y and

things I've _ done. I let my past go _ past, and now I'm hav-ing more fun. I'm let-ting

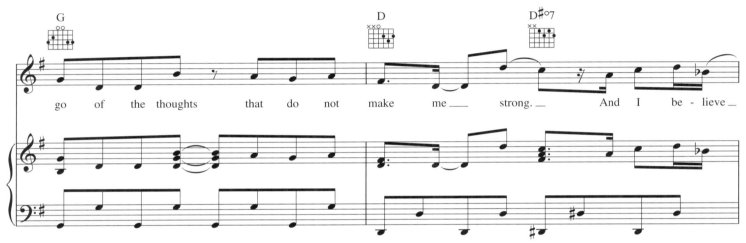

go of the thoughts that do not make me _ strong. _ And I be-lieve _

_ this way can feel the same for ev-er-y-one. And if I fall a-sleep, I _

D.S. al Coda I

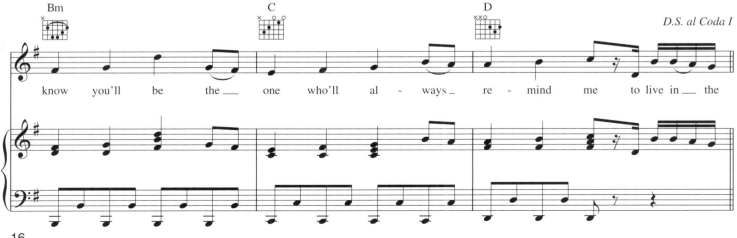

know you'll be the _ one who'll al-ways _ re-mind me to live in _ the

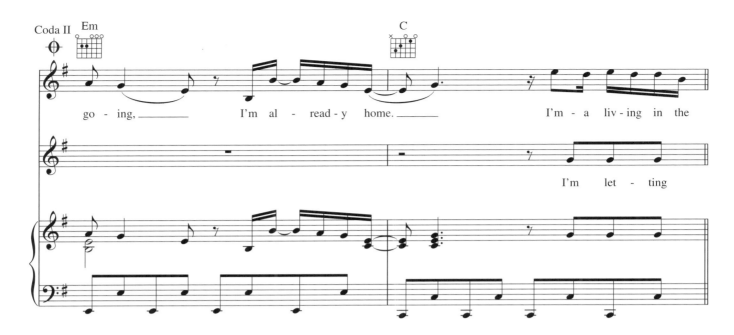

Coda II

go - ing, _____ I'm al - read - y home. _____ I'm - a liv - ing in the
I'm let - ting

mo - ment. _____ I'm - a liv - ing my life, _____ just tak - in' it _____
my - self _____ off _____ the hook for things I've _____ done. _____ I let my

eas - y _____ with peace _ in my mind. _____ Got peace _ in my
past go _____ past, and now I'm hav - ing more fun. I'm let - ting

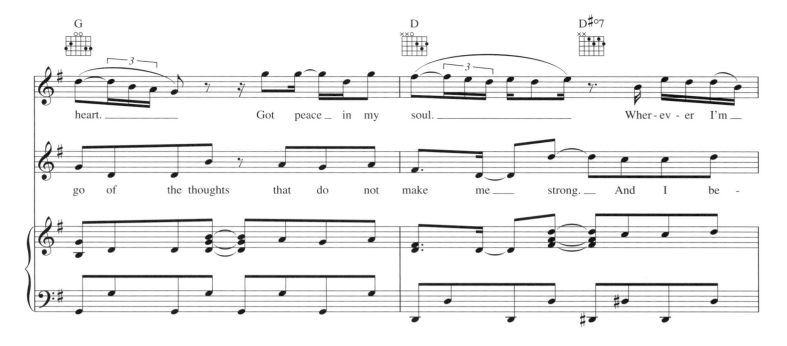

heart. _____ Got peace _ in my soul. _____ Wher - ev - er I'm _
go of the thoughts that do not make me _ strong. _ And I be -

go - ing, _____ I'm al - read - y home. _____ I'm - a liv - ing in the
lieve this way can feel the same for ev - er - y - one. I'm let - ting

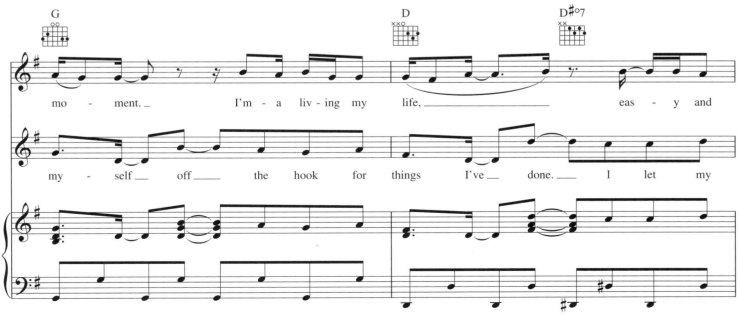

mo - ment. _ I'm - a liv - ing my life, _____ eas - y and
my - self __ off __ the hook for things I've _ done. _ I let my

breez - y with peace _ in my mind, with peace _ in my
past go _ past, and now I'm hav - ing more fun. I'm let - ting

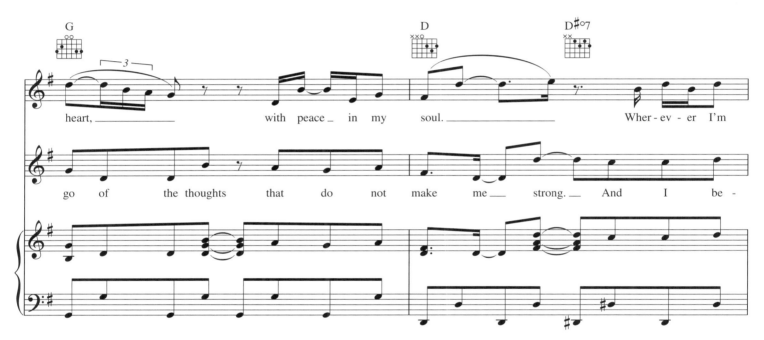

heart, _ with peace _ in my soul. _ Wher - ev - er I'm
go of the thoughts that do not make me _ strong. _ And I be -

go - ing, _ I'm al - read - y home. _ Liv - ing in the mo - ment.
lieve this way can feel the same for ev - er - y - one.

The Woman I Love

Words and Music by
Jason Mraz and David Hodges

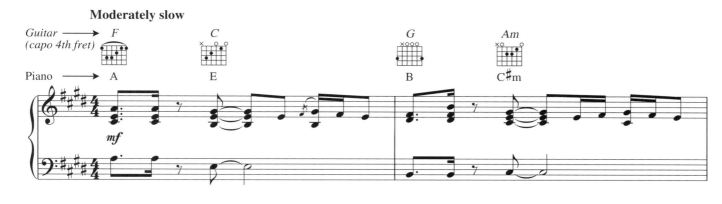

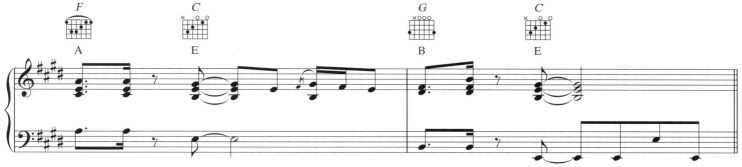

May-be I ig-nore___ you   with my___ choic - es.

Well, you an-noy___ me some-times   too with___ your___ voice,___

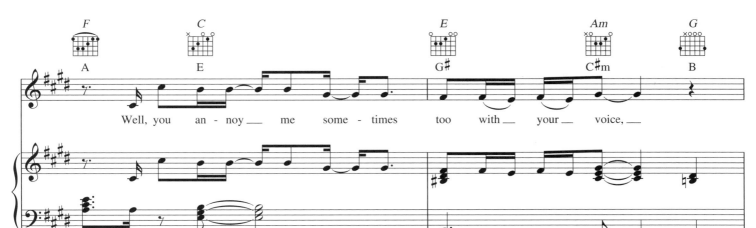

but that ain't e-nough for me ___ to move out and move ___ on. _____ I'm

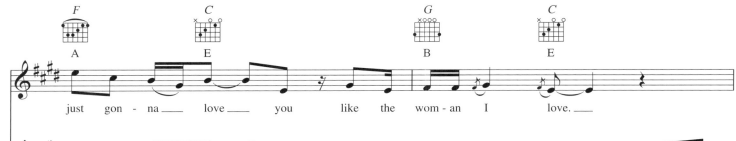

just gon-na ___ love ___ you like the wom-an I love. ___

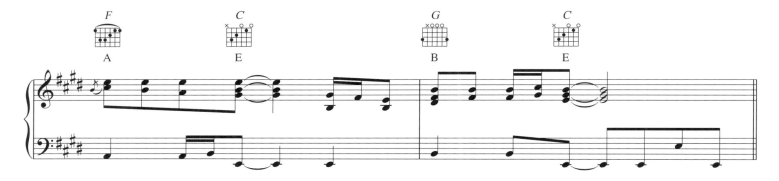

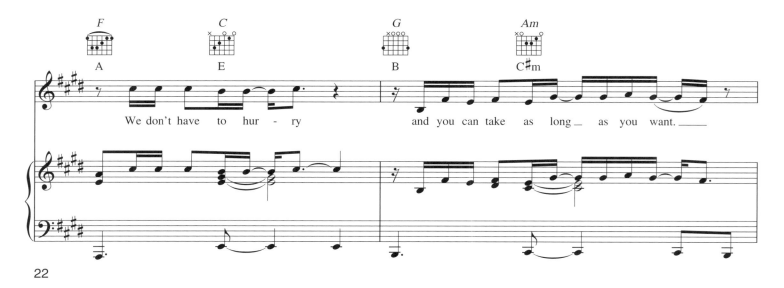

We don't have to hur-ry and you can take as long ___ as you want. ___

beat your-self ___ up; you let your-self ___ get ___ mad. ___ And in those

times when you stop lov-ing the wom-an I a-dore, ___ you can re-

lax, ___ be-cause, babe, I got ___ your back. ___ Mm, I got ___

___ you.

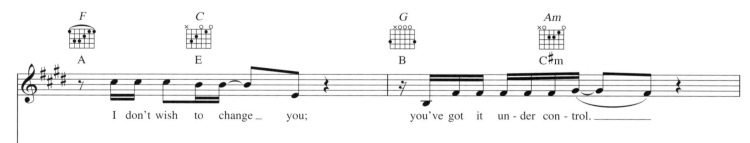

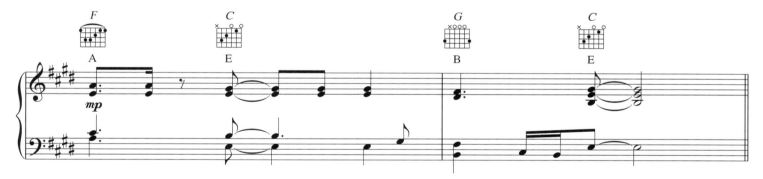

I don't wish to change _ you; you've got it un-der con-trol. _____

I'm gon-na___ love___ you. You're the wom-an I _____ love. ___

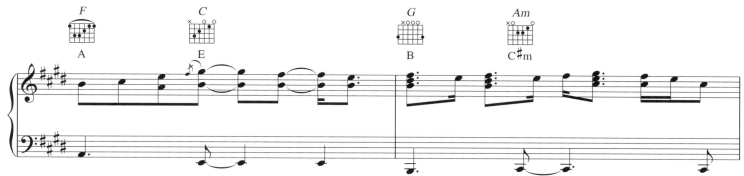

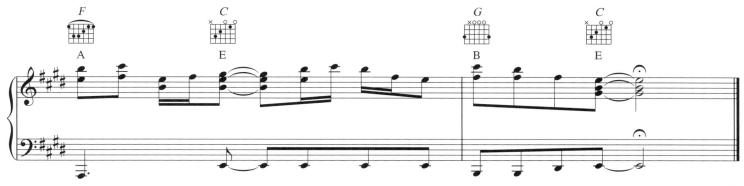

I Won't Give Up

Words and Music by
Jason Mraz and Michael Natter

*Guitarists: Tune 6th string down to D.

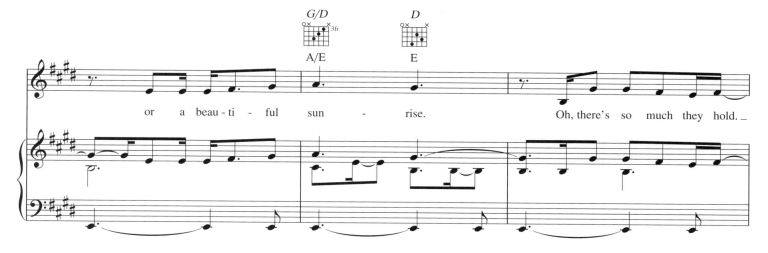

or a beau-ti-ful sun - rise. Oh, there's so much they hold. _

And just like them old _____ stars,

I see that you've come so ___ far _____ to be right where _

you are. How old is your soul? _____

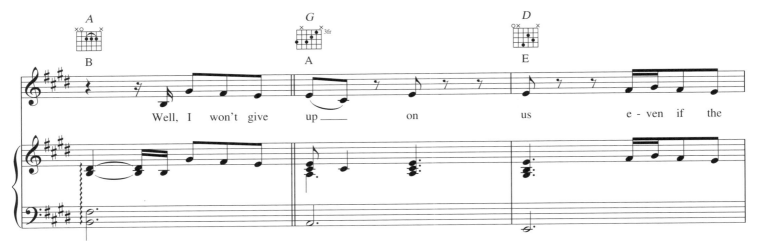

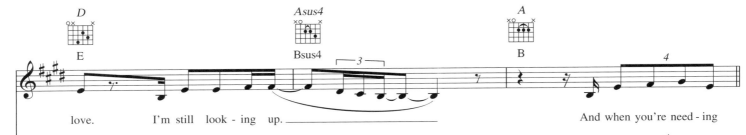

G/D   D
A/E   E

___ I'll be here pa - tient - ly wait - ing ___ to see what you

Asus4   A   G
Bsus4   B   A

find.   'Cause e - ven ___ the stars, ___ they

D   Bm7   A
E   C#m7   B

burn;   some e - ven fall ___ to the earth. ___ We got ___ a

G   D   Asus4
A   E   Bsus4

lot ___ to learn. God knows, we're worth ___ it. ___

No, ____ I ____ won't give up. ____ I don't

wan - na be some-one who walks a - way so eas - i - ly. I'm here to stay and make the dif - fer - ence that

I can make. _____ Our

dif - f'renc - es, they do a lot to teach us how to use the tools and gifts we got; yeah, we got a lot ____

5/6

Words and Music by
Jason Mraz and Michael Natter

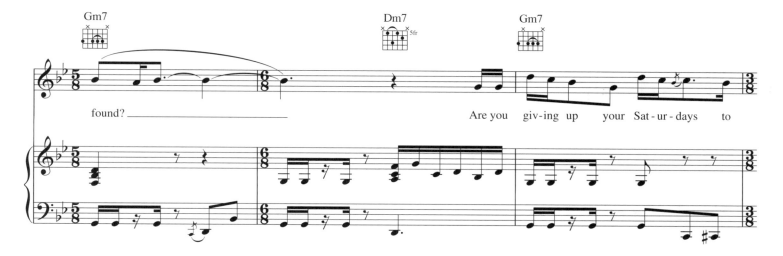

found? _____ Are you giv-ing up your Sat-ur-days to

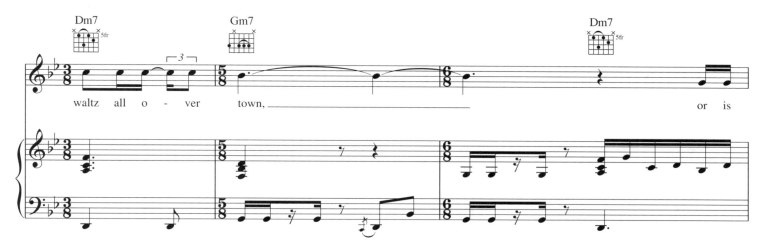

waltz all o-ver town, _____ or is

ev-'ry day a jol-ly hol-i-day __ with the Mar-y you're with now?

You can give it all ___ a-way, give it all ___ and be un-stop-pa-ble. ___

play.   Well, you can give it

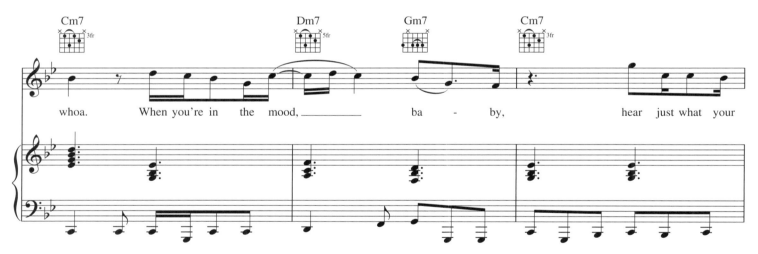

just   let   go. ___ Whoa, ___ whoa, ___ whoa, ___   whoa, ___ whoa, ___ whoa, ___ whoa, ___

whoa.   When you're in the mood, _____ ba - by,   hear just what your

heart has to say.   When the world is turn-ing top - side and   tur - vy, think you'd bet - ter

hur-ry down _____ to the bot-tom of your soul _____ and be

love. _____

Your _ word is your ac - cess, your mouth is your

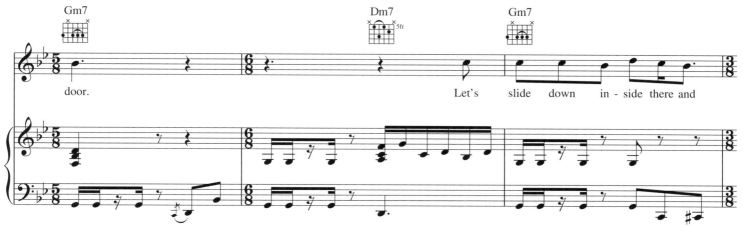

door. Let's slide down in - side there and

see what's in _____ store. _____ In the

mid-dle there's a rhy-thm kick-in'. It's a frig-gin' heart - beat _____ (beat,

beat, beat, beat). At the bot-tom, there's a lot of wa-ter keep-ing your

D.S. al Coda II

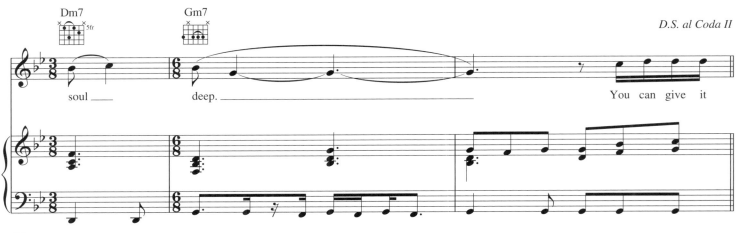

soul ___ deep. _____ You can give it

just let go. ___ Whoa, ___ whoa, ___ whoa, ___ w - w - w - whoa, ___ w - w - w - whoa, ___ whoa, ___

whoa.

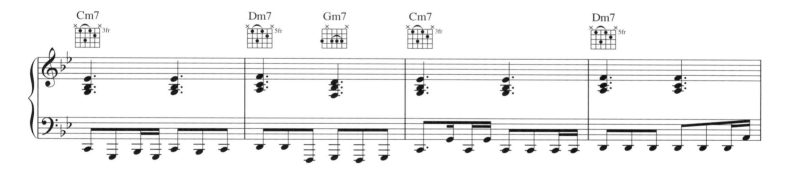

Yeah. _____ And when you're in a mood, _____ pret - ty ba - by, ___

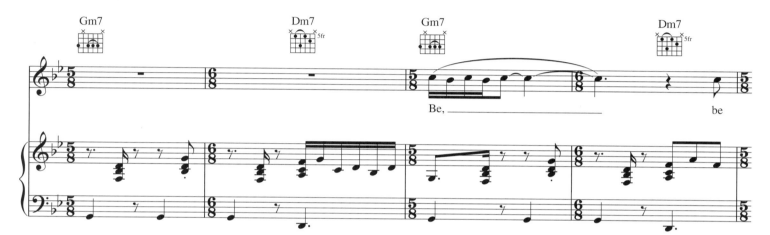

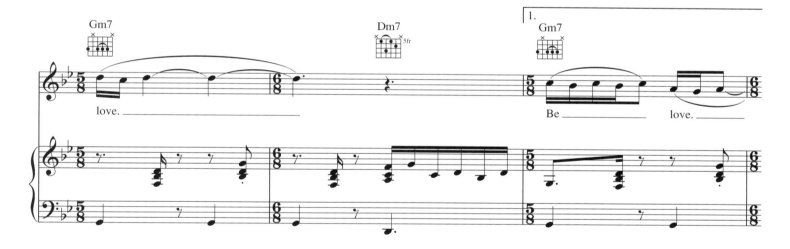

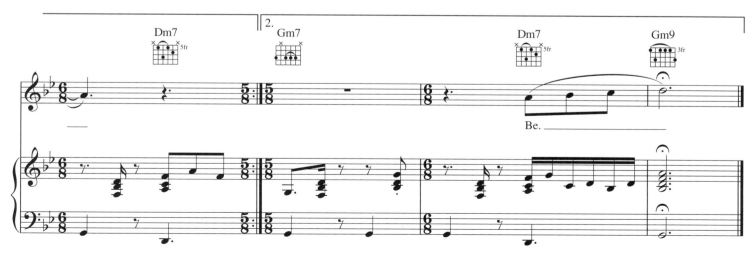

Everything Is Sound
(La La La)

Words and Music by
Jason Mraz, Matt Hales,
Mike Daly and Martin Terefe

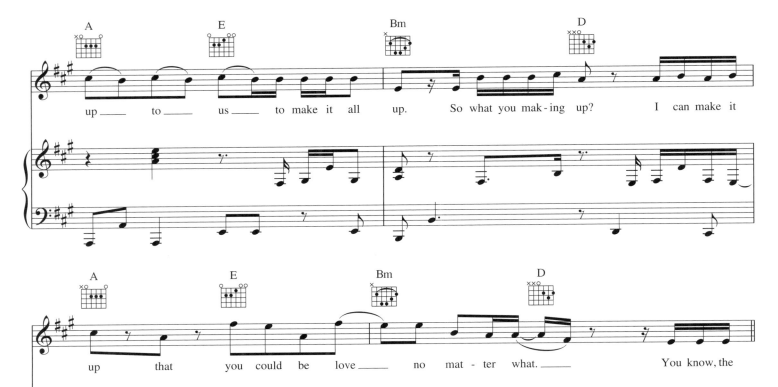

up ____ to ____ us ____ to make it all up. So what you mak-ing up? I can make it

up that you could be love ____ no mat-ter what. ____ You know, the

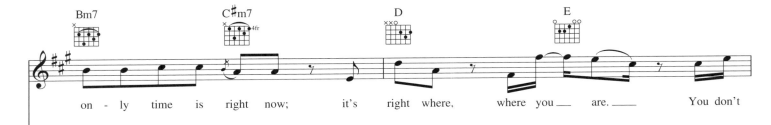

on - ly time is right now; it's right where, where you __ are. __ You don't

need a va-ca-tion ____ when there's noth-ing to es-cape __ from. Sing-ing... __

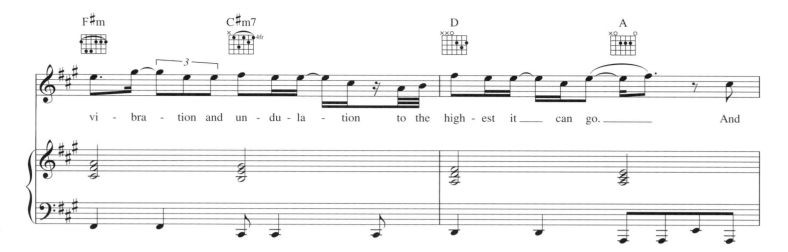

vi - bra - tion and un - du - la - tion to the high - est it ___ can go. ___ And

trust me, hear me. If it makes you wan - na sing, ___ just sing it...

sing. Ha, la, la, la, la, ___ la, la, ___ yeah. Ha, la, la, la, la, ___ la, let's all

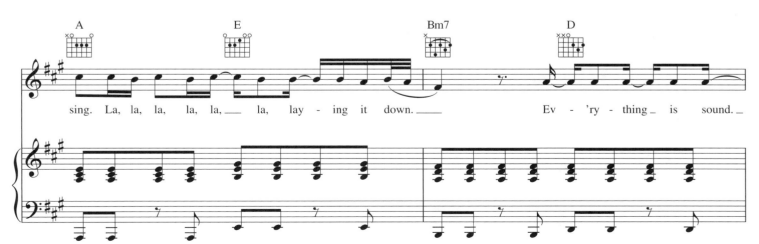

sing. La, la, la, la, la, ___ la, lay - ing it down. ___ Ev - 'ry - thing ___ is sound. ___

Ha-le-la-la-la - la-la, ___ yeah. Ha-le-la-la-la - la, let's all

To Coda ⊕

sing. Ha-le-la-la-la - la-le-lu - jah. ___ Well, it's a

song that I've for-got - ten of - ten. ___

It does-n't make me wrong, ___ 'cause we all need __ the dark-ness __

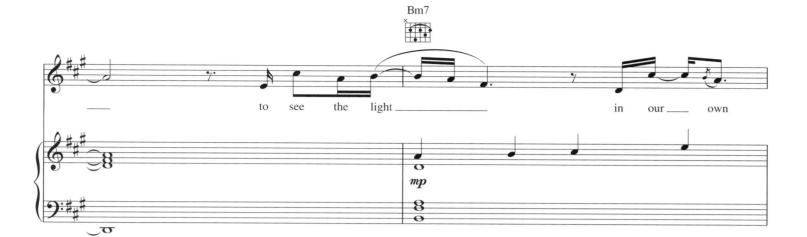

to see the light _____ in our _ own

D.S. al Coda

eyes. _____ Come on _ and sing it... _

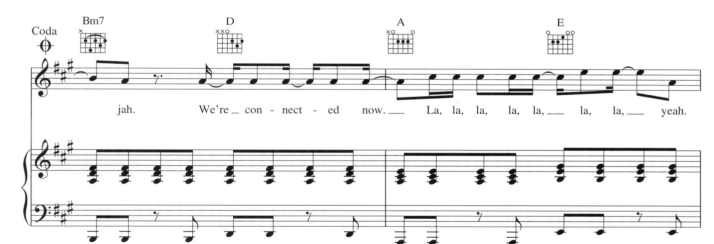

jah. We're _ con - nect - ed now. _ La, la, la, la, la, _ la, la, _ yeah.

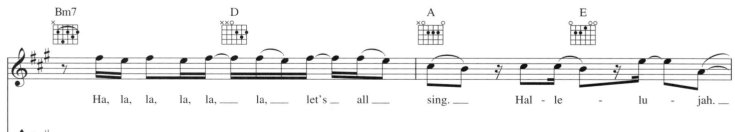

Ha, la, la, la, la, _ la, _ let's _ all _ sing. _ Hal - le - lu - jah. _

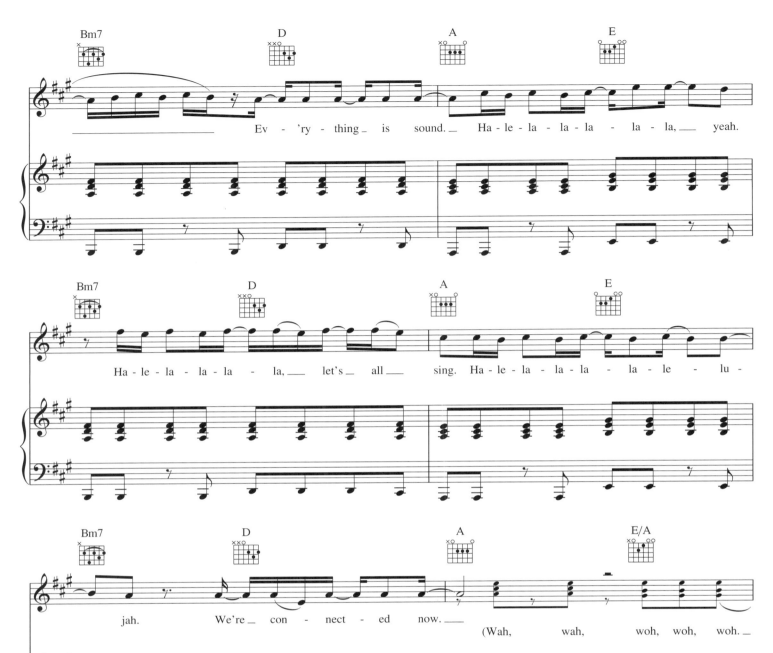

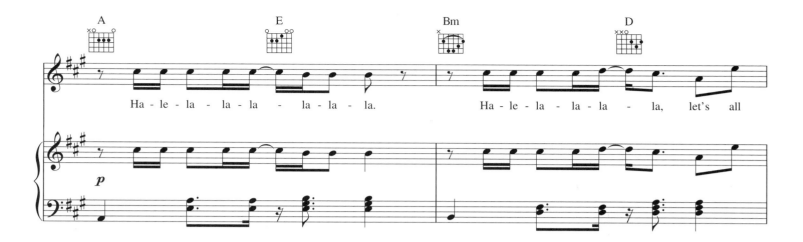

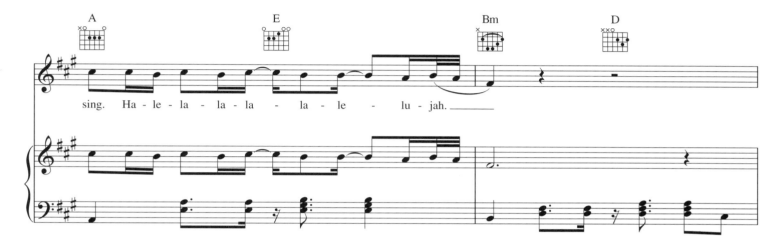

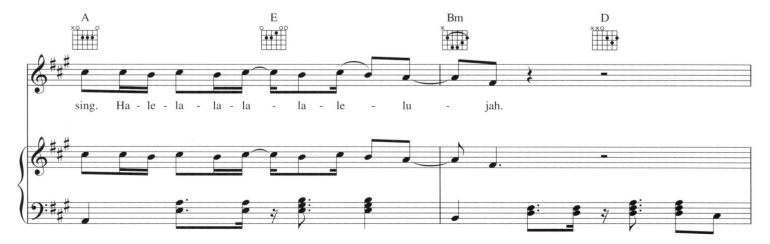

Ha-le-la-la-la - la-la, ___ yeah. Ha-le-la-la-la-la, ___ let's ___ all ___

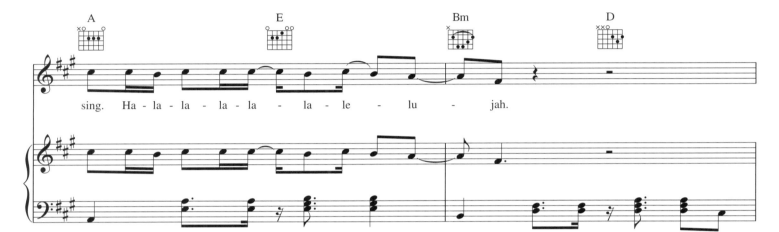

sing. Ha-la-la-la-la - la-le - lu - jah.

Ha-la-la-la-la - la-le-la, yeah. Ha-la-la-la-la - la-le-lu -

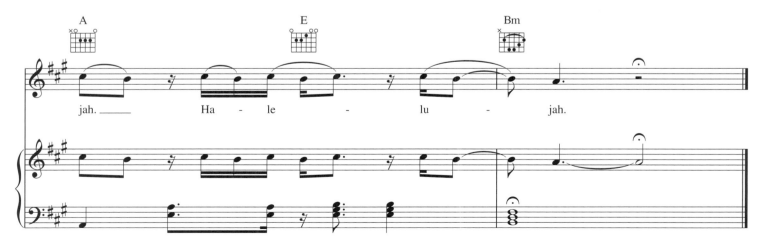

jah. ___ Ha - le - lu - jah.

93 Million Miles

Words and Music by
Jason Mraz, Michael Natter
and Mike Daly

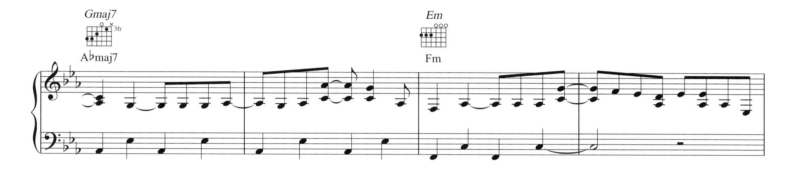

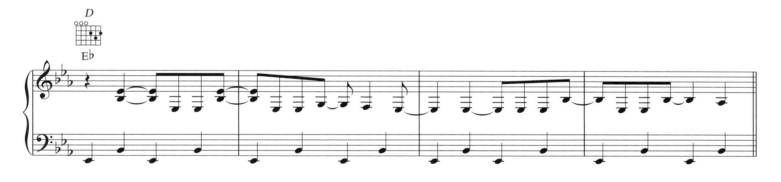

Nine-ty-three mil-lion miles __ from the sun. Peo- ple, get read- y, get read- y 'cause here it

*Guitarists: Tune 6th string down to D. Capo 1st fret (fret numbers next to chord diagrams indicate number of frets above capo).

you can al - ways _ come _ home." _

Two

hun - dred for - ty thou - sand miles _ from the moon. We've come a long way to be - long _

_ here to share this view of the night, a glo - ri - ous night. _ O - ver the ho - ri - zon is an-

Home.

Home. You can al - ways_ come_ back.

Ev - 'ry road is a slip-p'ry slope. _____ There is al - ways a hand

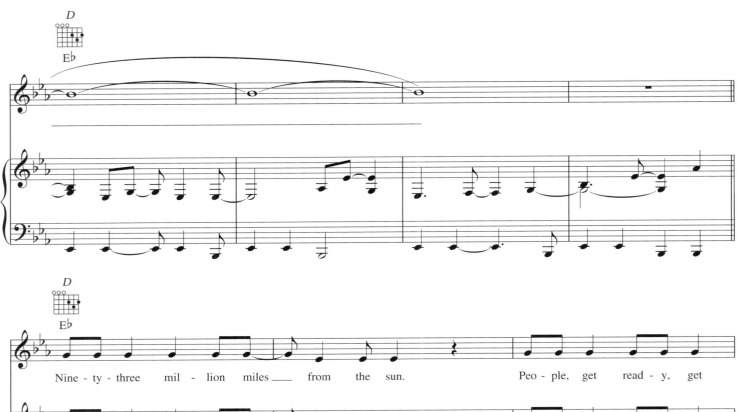

Nine-ty-three mil-lion miles __ from the sun. Peo-ple, get read-y, get

read-y 'cause here it comes. It's a light, a beau-ti-ful light, __ o-

ver the ho-ri-zon, in-to our eyes. _____

64

Frank D. Fixer

Words and Music by
Jason Mraz, Martin Terefe
and Sacha Skarbek

Moderately slow

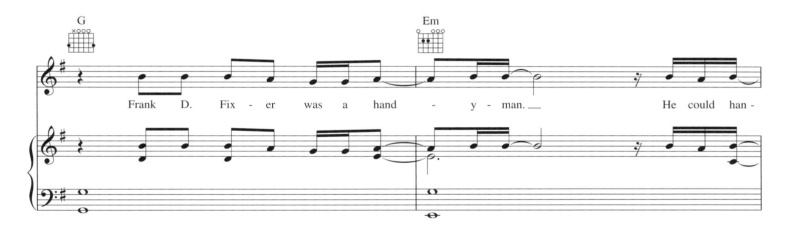

Frank D. Fix - er was a hand - y - man.___ He could han -

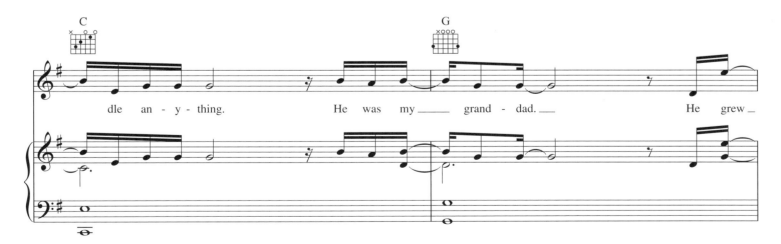

dle an - y - thing. He was my ___ grand - dad. ___ He grew ___

his own food _____ and he could fix his own _____ car. _____ I watched _____

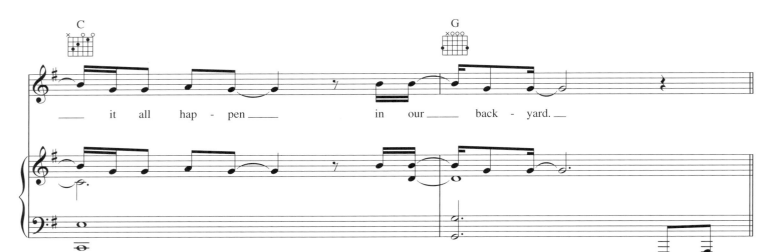

_____ it all hap - pen _____ in our _____ back - yard. _____

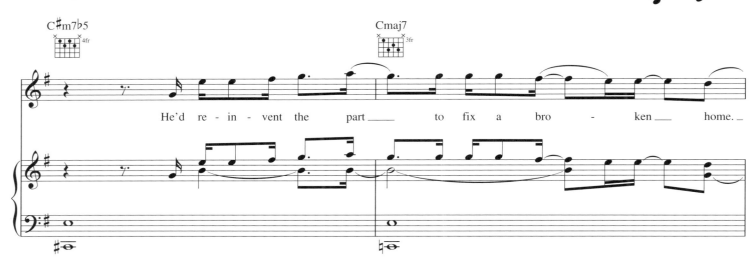

He'd re - in - vent the part _____ to fix a bro - ken _____ home.

_____ He'd re - store _____ the heart. _____

Well, if Frank D. Fix - er were a - live _____ to - day, _____ well, he might laugh _____

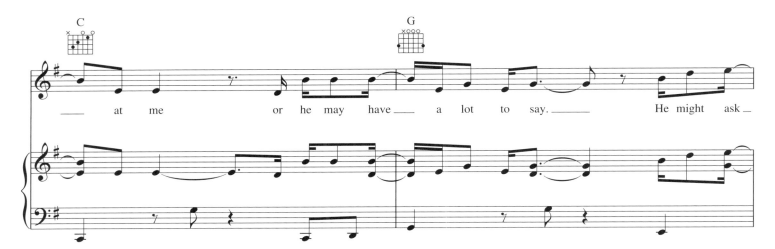

_____ at me or he may have _____ a lot to say. _____ He might ask _____

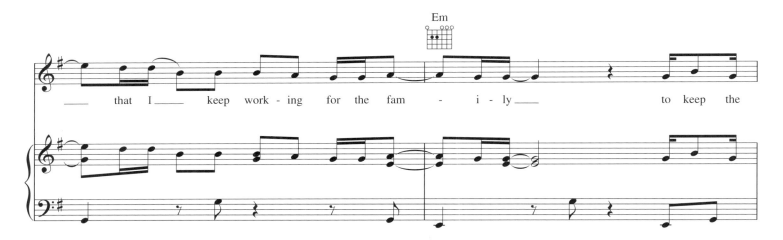

_____ that I _____ keep work - ing for the fam - i - ly _____ to keep the

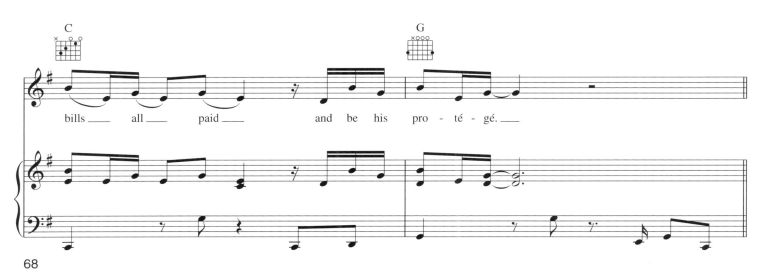

bills _____ all _____ paid _____ and be his pro - té - gé. _____

68

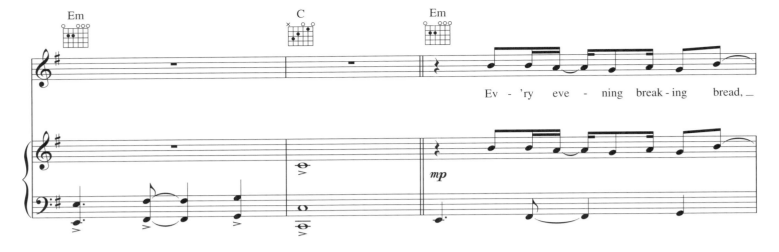

Ev - 'ry eve - ning break - ing bread, __

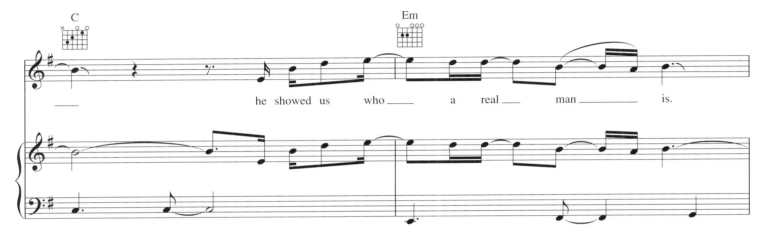

__ he showed us who __ a real __ man __ is.

No mat - ter what __ my grand - ma __ said, __ he would nev -

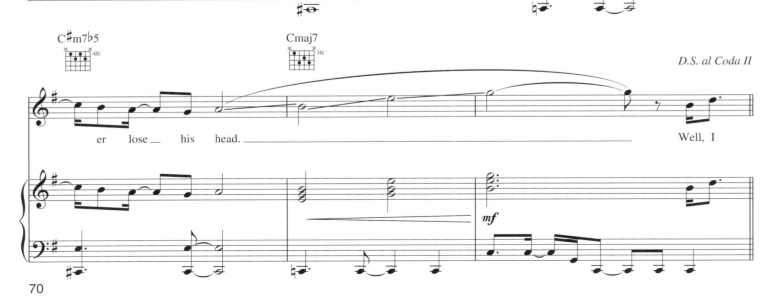

er lose __ his head. _____ Well, I

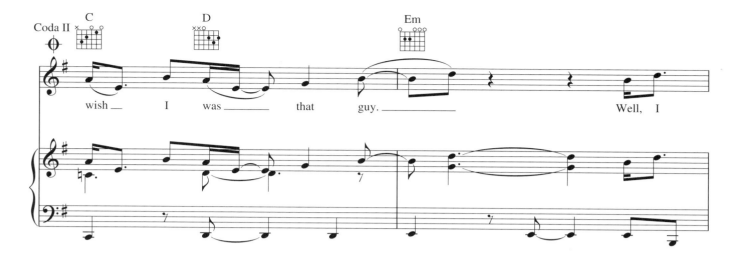

wish ___ I was ___ that guy. ___ Well, I

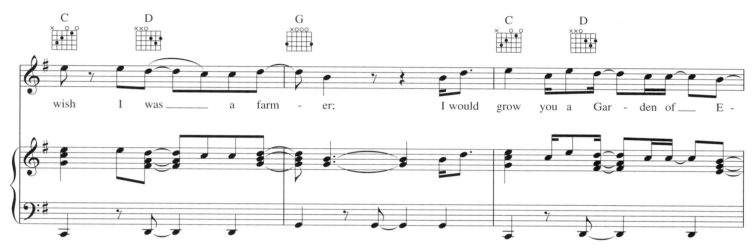

wish I was ___ a farm - er; I would grow you a Gar - den of ___ E -

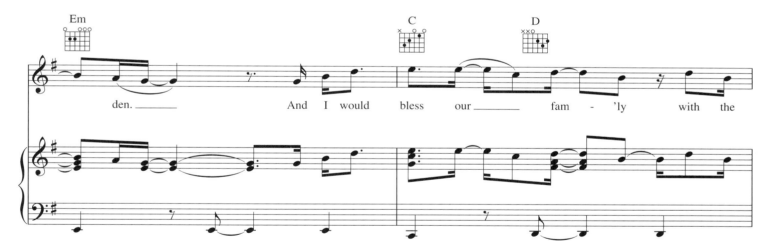

den. ___ And I would bless our ___ fam - 'ly with the

gifts that grand - dad hand - ed me. How won - der - ful ___ that would be. ___

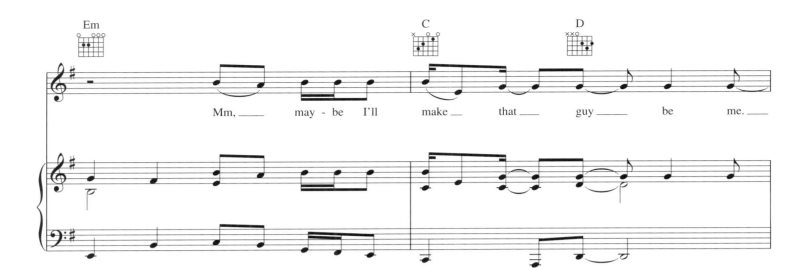

Mm, _____ may - be I'll make _____ that _____ guy _____ be me. _____

Play 4 times

Who's Thinking About You Now?

Words and Music by
Jason Mraz and Eric Hinojosa

*Recorded a half step lower.

Guitarists: Capo at 4th fret to play along with recording (fret numbers next to chord diagrams indicate number of frets above capo).

74

have - n't, well, they __ will. __ Ba - by, they all will. _____

__ Just __ when you sus - pect - ed life could - n't get hard - er, some -

thing comes a - long and makes your dark day dark - er. The weight of it all __ falls __ on

you. _____ Who __

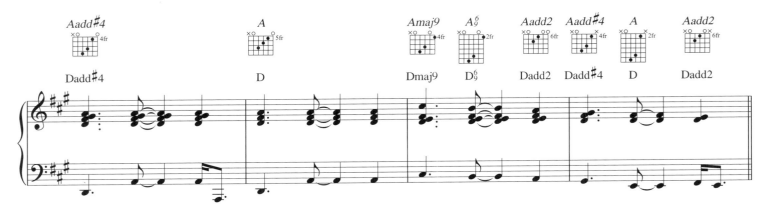

our two hands __ are linked to - geth - er with an am - per - sand, it's my __ kind of

In Your Hands

Words and Music by
Jason Mraz

*Recorded a half step lower.
Guitarists: Capo at 2nd fret to play along with recording.

So I'll leave it in your __ hands __ now to come _____ through. __

I'll leave it in your __ hands __ now to come _____ through. __

__ I like climb-ing a moun-tain or climb-ing

back in-to bed. _____ I love __ mak-ing break-fast __ for

So I'll leave it in your ___ hands ___

now to come ___ through. ___ I'll leave it in your ___ hands ___

now to come ___ through. ___ I'll leave it in your ___ hands ___

now to come ___ through. ___ {I'm gon - na / I'll} leave it in your ___ hands ___

Be Honest

Words and Music by
Jason Mraz and Michael Natter

Moderately

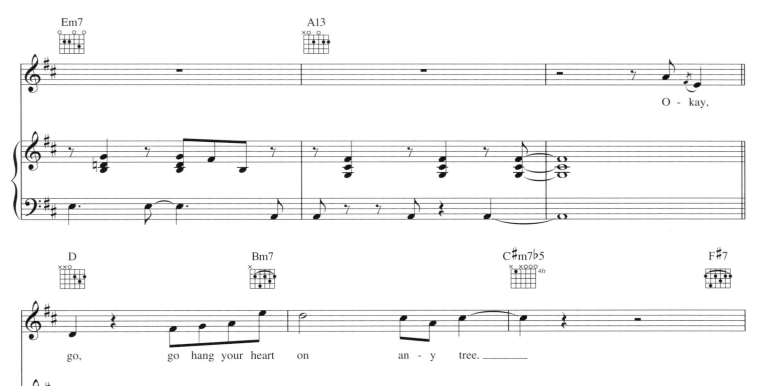

go,   go hang your heart on   an - y   tree. _____

O - kay,

You can make your-self a-vail-a-ble to an-y-bod-y, ___ 'cause

ev-'ry liv-ing per-son knows you are a prize. ___ Which-ev-er way you go, I'll be eas-

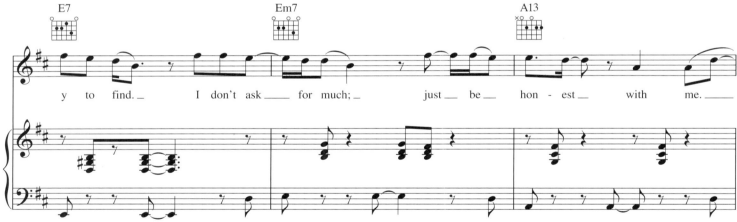

y to find. _ I don't ask ___ for much; _ just _ be _ hon-est ___ with me. ___

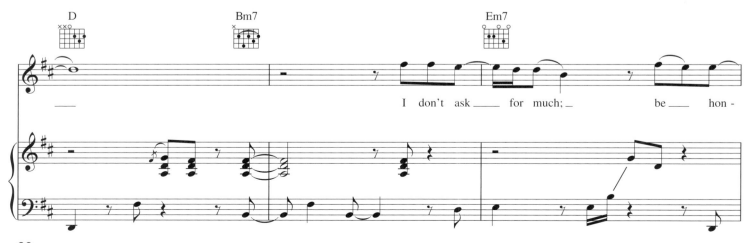

I don't ask ___ for much; _ be ___ hon-

est. _____ Think of this song as a prom - ise; you can do what you want. _

If you de - cide you want to move in - to a new stage, de -

let - ing me from pag - es in your mis - sion state - ment, my love is un - con - di - tion - al; make

no mis - take. _ I don't ask _ for much; _ just _ be _ hon - est _ with me. _____

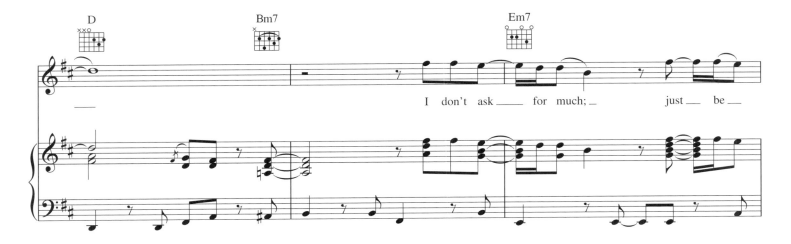

I don't ask ___ for much; ___ just ___ be ___

hon-est ___ with me. ___ Who we are ___ when

love is what it wants to be, ___ we are free ___ and we ___ are

hav-ing the best ___ day ev-er by far, be-ing treat-ed to the light like a

su - per - star.

I can hold space while you see what your heart

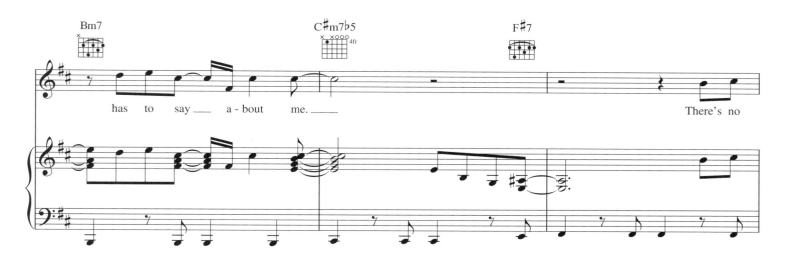

has to say ___ a - bout me. ___ There's no

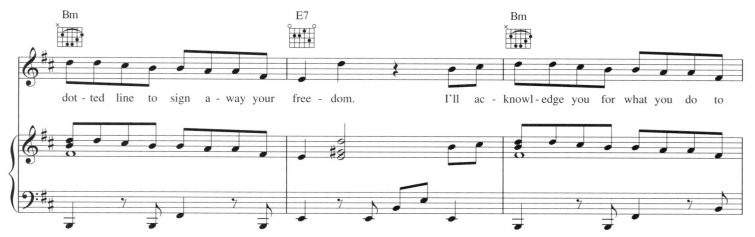

dot - ted line to sign a - way your free - dom. I'll ac - knowl - edge you for what you do to

keep strong. _____ I'll al-ways get be-hind you; don't get me wrong. _____ I don't ask _____

_____ for much; _____ just _ be _ hon-est _ with me. _____

I _____ don't ask _____ for much; _____ just _ be _ hon-est _ with me.

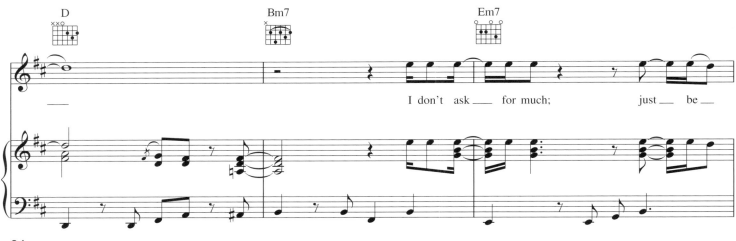

_____ I don't ask _____ for much; _____ just _ be _____

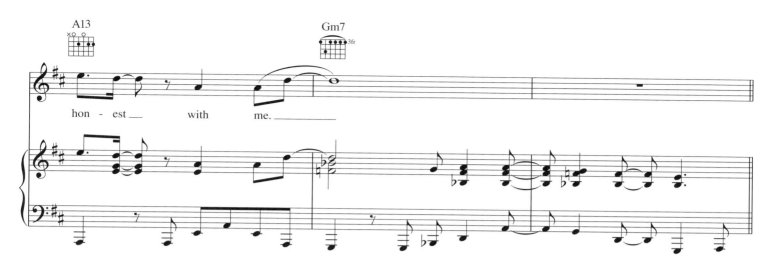

hon - est ___ with me. ___

Who we are ___ when love is what it wants to be, ___ we are free ___

___ and we ___ are ___ hav - ing the best ___ day ev - er by far. ___

Yes, we are. ___

The World As I See It

Words and Music by
Jason Mraz and Rick Nowels

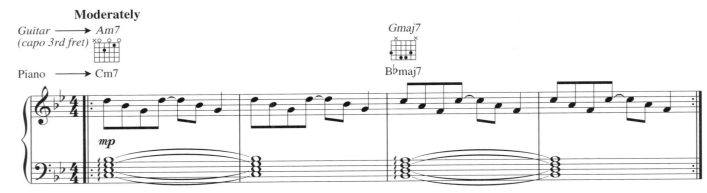

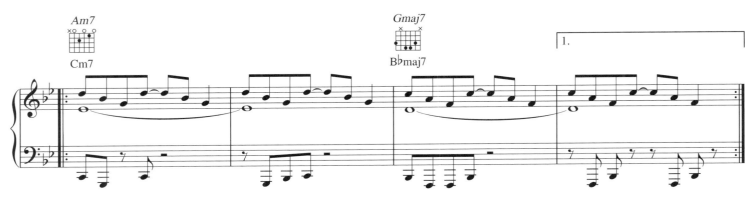

The world _____ as I see it is a re-mark-

a-ble place, ___ a beau-ti-ful house ___ in a

for me to love you. No, __ it's not a dif - fi - cult thing. __ It's not __ hard

for me to love you, hard __ for me to love you be - cause you are the world __ to me. __

Yeah, the world _____ as I __ see it is a re - mark-

a - ble place. __ Ev - 'ry man __ makes a

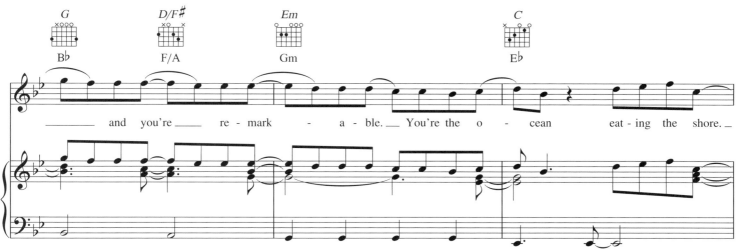

I'm Coming Over

Words and Music by
Jason Mraz and Mike Daly

ty through ten and a half __ thou - sand yes - ter - days. __

A wan - ing moon __ il - lu - mi - nates __ all the se - crets I've __ been keep -

ing and cast - ing off __ of my bal - co - ny. __ Oh, __

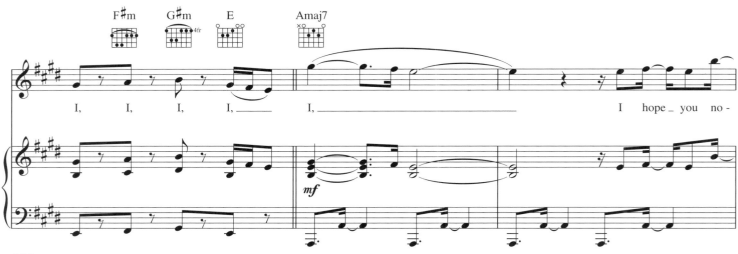

I, I, I, I, __ I, __ I hope __ you no -

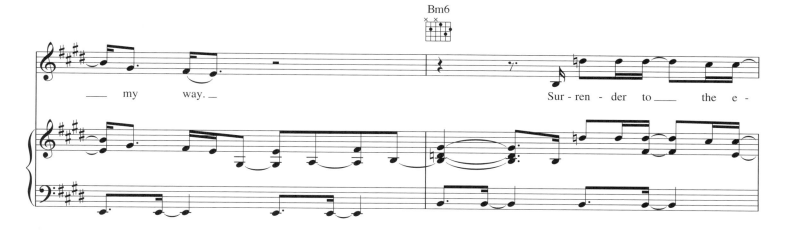

my way. ___ Sur - ren - der to ___ the e -

ter - nal - i - ty ___ of now, _____ and en - joy the mid - night

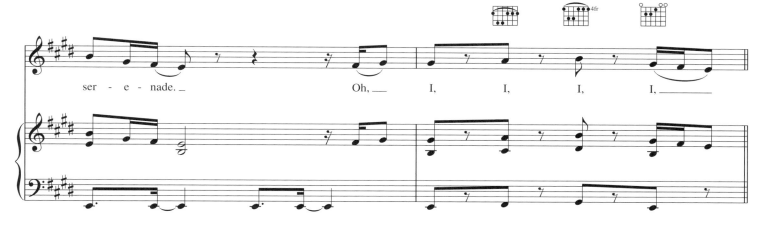

ser - e - nade. ___ Oh, ___ I, I, I, I, _____

I, _____ I hope ___ you no - tice _____

ver   just to   say good-night. __   I hope   you   no - tice __   I was nev-er o - ver you. __

To Coda ⊕

I   hope   you

no - tice __   I was nev-er o - ver you. _____   My

mind _____   is   run - ning,   but I _____   still   hear _____   the mu - sic all _____   a - round _____

me pro - found - ly. _____ I, I, I, I, _____

God, _____ I love _ this. If ev - er there _ was a place that I _____ could stay, _

_____ I found _ it. _____ I, I, I, I, _____

I, _____ I hope _ you no - tice, _____

my love._____ I'm com-ing o-

no - tice ____ I was nev - er o - ver you. ____

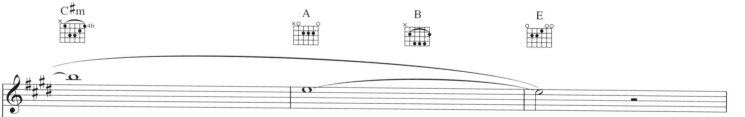

More Great Piano/Vocal Books

FROM CHERRY LANE

For a complete listing of Cherry Lane titles available, including contents listings, please visit our web site at

www.cherrylane.com